To Jordan

with all good wishes.
Hope you enjoy these
poems.

Stewart Henderson

Aug 2000
England

Who Left Grandad at the Chip Shop?
and other poems

To mws
who so deserves
to be a child

Who Left Grandad at the Chip Shop?

and other poems

STEWART HENDERSON

Illustrations by
Nigel Baines

LION
Children's Books

Published by
Lion Publishing plc
Sandy Lane West, Oxford, England
www.lion-publishing.co.uk
ISBN 0 7459 4412 4

First edition 2000
10 9 8 7 6 5 4 3 2 1 0

A catalogue record for this book is available
from the British Library

Typeset in 12/16 ITC Century Book
Printed and bound in Great Britain by
Biddles Ltd, Guildford and King's Lynn

Contents

Me
and my
world

Who left Grandad at the chip shop?

'Who left
Grandad at the chip shop?
Who poured
syrup down the sink?
Which one
left the freezer open?
Why don't
any of you think?

Why's the
rabbit in the wardrobe?
How did
Marmite get up there?
What's this
melted biro doing?
Don't you know
that socks should pair?

When's this
filthy games' kit needed?
Where's the
barbecue fork gone?' –
Our house
is a haze of questions,
best not
answer every one.

Sporting delusions

I'm a panther
I'm an acrobat
I'm an athlete so supreme
I'm a spinning ballerina
I'm a Herculean dream.

I'm a supple tightrope walker
I am loose-limbed
I'm so fit
I am bendy, bouncy, leapy
every single bit.

I also have my off days
as I stand here on the line
I'm a small and tearful goalie
and, so far, I've let in nine.

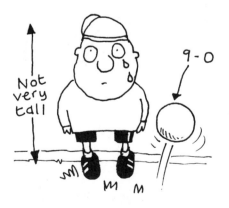

Sweet and sour

I'm trying so hard to like celery,
it's not a great favourite of mine,
how can it be wholesome and eatable
when it tastes of wood chippings and twine?

So MmmmYum for chocolate egg sandwiches,
when they get to your tummy, they glows,
oh wonder, oh marvel, oh miracle.
How the hen does it, nobody knows.

School gate protector

There's a being who is fearsome
she's also short and stout.
Her face is stern with firmness
and twice a day she's out

to guard the zebra crossing
and halt traffic with a glare.
All juggernauts are powerless
at her piercing, peak-capped stare.

At rush hour she is ominous
for everyone must wait
and even gloss Ferraris
dare not accelerate.

Police cars, buses, cyclists
all quiver in the road
and woe betide the scuffed, white van
with crammed, uneven load.

All vehicles brake to worship her
they dip their lights half-beam
yet still her shapeless mac shines out,
a sort of grubby cream.

The secret of her mighty rule
is a spindly, spellbound prop.
It's her magic wand of yellow –
a metal lollipop.

My cousin

My cousin is a nuisance,
my cousin is a brat,
his face is round
and also square
triangular and flat.

My cousin's very ugly,
he's also rather short,
he's scabby
and unsightly,
my cousin is a wart.

My cousin's always silent,
he follows me around
this small
and shaking creature
who never makes a sound.

My cousin often visits
he lives quite far away,
in Cheshire,
with his father.
His mother died last May.

My cousin's so disruptive,
I'm so glad when he's gone,
it's difficult
to sleep
when the light is always on.

Sometimes

Sometimes I don't like myself
but then sometimes I do,
and sometimes it's so hard to know
if what I feel is true.

Like when I have a tantrum,
is that all people see?
I'm only like that sometimes,
that fury's not all me.

Sometimes, I go racing through
the playground in my head,
which is awkward if I should
be doing geography instead.

Those 'sometimes' I go missing
while my body is still here,
they're much the best of sometimes –
that's when I disappear.

For then I go all over
from Ecuador to Mars,
to nesting with the eagle
and swapping round the stars.

That magic sometimes when I feel
beyond the moon and free,
the sometimes I forget myself
and let myself be me.

I'm trying to yodel

I'm trying to yodel
as I yo-yo my throat.
I gulp up and down
without making a note.

How do the Swiss do it,
and the Austrians too?
Did you know it's the Swiss
who make clocks go 'cuckoo'?

They are brilliant at sounds,
yet my yodel's quite dead.
Think I'll water it down,
and just gargle instead.

I drive my mother potty

I drive my mother potty
I drive her up the wall
I drive her barmy, batty,
berserk, and that's not all.

I drive my mother bonkers
I'm really not sure how
She says I drive her loco
So I drive her Spanish now.

I drive my mother crazy
I drive her much too far
I wish she'd drive me
– home from school –
but we haven't got a car.

Rest assured?

Yesterday my mother
was speaking
on the 'phone to somebody.

I don't know
who it was,
possibly God
or someone in government
because she said
'it is very important
in all this
that you rest a shore'.

Today
I am at the beach
doing my bit
in trying
to rest a shore.

Saying to the sand
'it must be so tiring
entertaining
the clinking waves all day
and then
being kept up
at night
by the bright, partying moon.'

So I didn't
bring my frisbee
or bucket and spade.
I heard what my mother said,
she sounded quite serious,
because it's very important
to rest a shore.

Bon-fire night

It's Bon-fire night
it's Bon-fire night
when night is bright
and crackling with de-light
Guy looks a sight
a darkening plight
his trousers charred
and waistcoat far too tight
It's Bon-fire night
when rockets might
land on Ben Nevis
that's the height of flight
On Bon-fire night
on Bon-fire night
the flames' red jaws
are wide to bite the night
It's Bon-fire night...

*(Repeat again, this time a
bit louder)*

Forecast

When January howls,
especially in May,
and leaves are turning brown –
can June be far away?

If it's snowing in July,
is Nature out to fool yer?
It's as my grandma says,
'the weather's most peculiar'.

The Nothing Crew

We like doing nothing
and nothing's what we do.
By being good for nothing –
that's how our talent grew.
We hang around in precincts
and padlocked swing-parks too,
we're ace at being nothing
'cos we're The Nothing Crew!

There's skateboard gangs
and Game Boy boys,
there's break-dance lads
making techno noise –
there goes a poser
on his racing bike –
well all that stuff
we don't like, 'cos...

We like doing nothing
and nothing's what we do.
By being good for nothing –
that's how our talent grew.
We hang around in precincts
and padlocked swing-parks too,
we're ace at being nothing
'cos we're The Nothing Crew!

There's scratch-card kids
out on the cadge
but, *'we have nothing'*
is our badge.
Graffiti posse's
spray-can touch
is never going
to grab us much.

Computer geeks
they make no sound
and some still have
a paper round,
and then there's
channel surfing nerds –
remote-controlled
but lost for words, 'cos...

We like doing nothing
and nothing's what we do.
By being good for nothing –
that's how our talent grew.
We hang around in precincts
and padlocked swing-parks too,
we're ace at being nothing
'cos we're The Nothing Crew!

Homework

Bash the cymbals
and the drums
brush the chimes
I've done my sums

Close the curtains
dim the light
go to bed
not one is right

Water
world

What is the point of a goldfish?

What is the point of a goldfish?
What is it exactly they do?
They're not very fast
and don't often last
you can't even put them in stew.

What is the use of a goldfish?
Their open mouths make them look dim.
It's a tedious fact
that their sole daily act
consists of a half-hearted swim.

What is the crux of a goldfish?
Would they like to discover new seas?
Or get up at dawn
and race round the lawn
and feel what it's like to have knees?

Would they like to shout 'boo' at the postman?
And bark at the starlings outside?
Or swallow the cat
thus becoming quite fat
and know what it's like to be wide?

What is the mark of a goldfish?
It's not like they do as they're told.
It lacks any goal
but this fortunate soul
just woke up one day and was gold.

... it all comes out in the wash

Oh yes, it all comes out in the wash:
pennies from pockets, rather rattly
a library ticket, rather unreadable
a tissue, rather everywhere
a battery, rather corroded
a water pistol, rather annoying
a mermaid, rather long hair
the breath of whales, rather overpowering.

Oh yes, it all comes out in the wash:
a vegetarian shark, rather unusual
a Spanish galleon, rather sunken
a tidal wave, rather frightening
a surfboard from 'Home And Away',
rather limited as an actor
a fun splash, rather expensive
King Canute's slippers, rather wet
submarine droppings, rather they hadn't.

Oh yes, it all comes out in the wash:
a sea shanty, rather bearded
the *Marie Celeste*, rather empty
a dolphin's joke book, rather smiley
several footprints, rather puzzling
a walrus's toothbrush, rather bristly
an oil-slick, rather awful
the Loch Ness Monster's photo album of humans,
rather grainy.

Oh yes, it all comes out in the wash:
a frozen pond, rather slippy
a whirlpool, rather gluggy
the Bermuda Triangle, rather pointed
a gondola, rather romantic
Niagara Falls, rather deafening
a solo voyage, rather on your own
driftwood, rather a hazard.

Oh yes, it all comes out in the wash...
... you should see the state of our washing
machine.

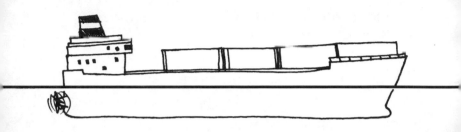

When you're a whale

When you're a whale
there is one place to be
and the deeper you go
then the deeper you'll see

That's why we go deeper
deep down we receive
the sense that we're special
deep down we believe

But up on the surface
are oil-slicks and ships
with bombs that are programmed
by small microchips

We don't tarry long there
we breach then we dive
deep to the depths
where our souls are alive

There we sing to each other
in deep liberty
it is as if heaven
is under the sea

And the deeper we go
the less that we doubt
we are spirits in waiting
whom you can't fathom out

Star potential

I know a quivering creature
who does things for a dare.
Extremely daft deeds really
so odd in one so spare.

There's not much substance to him
no tuned-up muscle tones,
no feats of strength, in fact, no feet,
or solid pelvic bones.

It could have been so different
had he been born with wings
but as it is he has this trait –
he tends to slide off things.

He's runny and he's gooey
quite lacking hair and teeth,
if asked to sit down on a chair
he ends up underneath.

So what he's done, he's taken
this tendency to slide
and made it an advantage
so now he slides world-wide.

He's slid the slopes of Aspen
where film stars go to play,
he's slid the Cresta Run, with no
helmet, Bob or sleigh.

He's climbed up Table Mountain,
this spineless little chap
and bungee-jumped straight off the top
which made him twang and flap.

Though sliding is his forte
he's learned another trade
it's being thrown through windows
and landing sort of splayed.

He wants to be in movies
I hope he gets his wish
But is there any call for
a stuntman jellyfish?

Secret friend

I have a secret friend
who glistens, swirls and laps,
who's older than the oldest bone,
well travelled, wise, perhaps
I'll ask her if she knows you,
you're by yourself, like me,
then we could go together
to our secret friend, the Sea.

Imaginary
world

The Trundle

The Trundle is a creature
who trundles everywhere
from Glasgow down to Cornwall
then up to Berkeley Square

He trundles over bridges
holding a balloon
he trundled once to Burma
but he shrunk in a monsoon

He trundles across meadows
in his polished shoes
he mumbles as he trundles
past stationary queues

He trundles at a steady pace
but if he's eating fudge
his trundling gets slower
then trundle turns to trudge

He trundles with a purpose
not knowing where he'll go
he doesn't know the difference
between Banbury Cross and Bow

The Trundle doesn't wear a watch
hc's always missing meals
he likes trundling in sewers
as the scenery appeals

So should you go to Rotherham
via the Pacific Rim
make sure you meet the Trundle
and start trundling with him

Behind the skirting board

What's that scratching?
behind the skirting board
scurrying and hurrying
behind the skirting board.

Is there more than one of them?
I'd rather there was none of them
what a weird phenomenon
behind the skirting board.

I'd like to think it's just a mouse
behind the skirting board
nibbling and scribbling
behind the skirting board.

What if it is something more
with spiky horns that pierce and gore?
I think I need a matador
behind the skirting board.

When at last it's bedtime
behind the skirting board
mysterious and serious
behind the skirting board.

With quiet rooms where monsters think
it's where the Cyclops learns to blink
the shadows are completely pink
behind the skirting board.

The weather's very different
behind the skirting board
tingaling and springaling
behind the skirting board.

Labradors clear up their mess
it's known as an elite address
where cold volcanoes convalesce
behind the skirting board
behind the skirting board
behind the skirting board.

Gullabull

Gullabull
is broad of heart
and chest and horns
and wings;
he follows trawlers,
surfs with clouds
and wears
enormous rings
right through his nose
where steam comes out,
his nostrils are colossal
but no one's yet seen
Gullabull
or even found his fossil.

He likes wild wastes
and mountain crags,
he grazes
and he flies.
Some experts say that
Gullabull
is just a pack of lies.
I know he's not,
I heard him
on the heathered
Isle of Mull.
And from the heights
he cried to me
'I AM GULLABULL.'

Auntie Diluvian and Uncle Orang

Auntie Diluvian and
Uncle Orang
are strange,
fascinating and sweet.
Auntie is shrivelled
and mumbles all day
whilst Uncle
likes picking his feet.

Auntie's wild stories
enthral me, and yet
my family believes
not a word.
But I know
she once
punched a dinosaur,
and also met Richard III.

Uncle is quieter
with very long arms,
most skilled in
the naming of trees.
And when we're asleep
he sits on the fridge
peacefully
sucking his fleas.

Auntie draws pictures
of things that she's seen,
of crossbows,
of floods and stampedes.
She hand-reared a dodo
and also a clown
by feeding them
lollipop seeds.

Uncle is ready
to help with odd jobs,
his favourite is
sweeping up leaves.
And if he wore clothes,
from the way that he walks
he'd always be
trailing his sleeves.

Even in sunlight
Auntie smells damp
with steam coming off
her old coat.
She blames that on Noah
for sailing too soon,
that, and a
very full boat.

Uncle is stringy,
thoughtful, serene,
his fur
a continuing flame.
He's also forgetful,
and loses things like
the disappeared half
of his name.

Auntie Diluvian
and Uncle Orang
enjoy playing
musical chairs.
But when it rains hard
Auntie goes quiet
whilst Uncle hides
under the stairs.

Let loose

Come let us draw,
with zero rules,
asteroids in hats
every gran in Pakistan
and an octopus in spats.

Come let us paint
majestic shapes,
the bumble of the bee
every brand new kangaroo
and the centre of the sea.

Come let us roam
the universe,
seek its unmarked core
by way of here we can get near
the rainbow's secret door.

Squishy and Squashy

Squishy and Squashy
have changeable shapes
in the forest
that nobody's seen.
They are spongily small
and waddle-like, wide
they are flubby
and tubby, and lean.

Squishy and Squashy
have flexible beds
which get weeny
and slighter and bigger.
They are matchbox minute
and continent huge
adapting to
whatever figure.

Squishy and Squashy
are rather like us
inasmuch
as they try to belong
by turning themselves
into what is required.
Be it short
or impossibly long.

But Squishy and Squashy
often return
to the forest
that nobody's seen
where the bluebells
are bluer than bluebells should be
and Spring
is beyond belief green.

There, Squishy and Squashy,
their own shapes again,
not ones that they think
they should be,
are able to change
into patterns and dreams
in the forest
where all shapes agree.

taking steps

watch out! take heed!
though still, beware!
a crocodile
upon the stair.

but a moving danger
even greater –
an alligator
on an escalator.

Animals,
birds,
reptiles and
crawlies...
world

Owl in the night

Owl in the night
owl in the night
soundless and searching
with
night vision sight
shrews, voles and dormice
can't offer much fight
when it's
swooping to feast,
an
owl in the night.

Owl in the night
owl in the night
with your own
Christmas carol
called Silent Flight;
the grey owl is grey
the snowy's so white.
What's that
making no sound?
An
owl in the night.

hummingbird

hummingbird
special role
shades and pastels
in its soul

busy life
daily chores
nectar-bearing
Santa Claus

deep at night
heartbeat slows
you would never know
it rose

with the sun
to the wing
spends its heart
on hovering

hummingbird
gifted one
plants a flower
where there's none

A hard life

Chomp the bookcase
chomp things pine
chomp Swedish seats
which·can recline.

Chomp elm and oak
and picture rails
chomp the desk
but not the nails.

Chomp the wardrobe
if it's yew
chomp 'til I
can barely chew.

Chomp the table
chomp the chairs
chomp the drawers,
they're like eclairs.

Chomp on top
and underneath –
I don't get splinters
in my teeth.

Scrunch and crunch
and munch the door,
a woodworm's life
is bore, then gnaw.

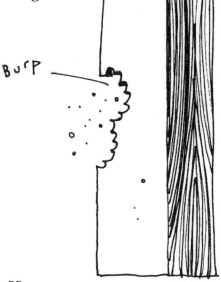

BURP

Table for one

A slug in a restaurant
is an upsetting sight
as its earth lips surround
bits it can bite.

Delia, Ainsley
Loyd Grossman too
all scream like a blender
if a slug starts to chew.

Who took its booking?
And then said, 'Of course,
we can do a twig pie
with mulched manure sauce.'

A slug's table manners
add up to none,
and a slug with a napkin
doesn't fool anyone.

Yet a slug doesn't bite,
chew, dine or pick.
For a slug 'slubs' its grub
which makes everyone sick.

(To 'slub' is a sound
which shouldn't be heard,
and if heard, best forgotten,
it's a loud, scary word.)

And when nothing is left
in the slug's china bowl
it asks for the bill
and 'slubs' it down whole.

Hysterical chorus

We're glad we're hyenas
instead of giraffes
we're nature's born comics
and life's one long laugh

We laugh when it's sunny
we laugh when it snows
we laugh when the thorn bush
scratches our nose

We laugh at each other
we laugh at the moon
we laugh through the haze
of a long afternoon

We laugh for an hour
and have a good lick
then listen to parrots
and laugh ourselves sick

We laugh at safaris
that camera-clad race
we laugh at their clothes
which look so out of place

We point at the zebra
and laugh 'til we weep
and chimpanzees tell us
we laugh in our sleep

Workers' paradise

the hammer-headed shark
the chisel-snouted hog
the fuse-wire watersnake
the spirit-level frog

the pliers scorpion
all vacancies are filled
the Allen-key giraffe –
creation's multi-skilled

Own private
world

If I were a duck

If I were a duck
I'd probably wear slippers,
but with my splayed-out feet
perhaps it should be flippers.

Yet if I were a goat
with horns and muddy soles,
I think I'd buy a hat,
ideally one with holes.

Rocking horse

Back and forth
back and forth
staying put
aiming north
forth and back
forth and back
polished neck
fastened tack

rearing up
cradle ride
wooden hooves
dappled hide

cantering
whilst staying home
hand-carved
equine
metronome

back and forth
forth and back
saddle dreams
nursery hack

World beater

Denis plays tennis
James goes to gym
Walter's a vaulter
I'm nothing like him

Bertha's a surfer
afflicted with cramps
I prefer licking
so I collect stamps

Sounds

Crunching ginger biscuits
is like hearing soldiers tread,
marching over gravel
on the inside of your head.

Chewing a marshmallow
is nowhere near as loud.
It's the smaller, sweet equivalent
of swallowing a cloud.

Watching, waiting

Teddy doesn't talk much
but it's his considered view
that everything now broken
has a chance to be made new.

And Teddy's magic wish
is, one multi-coloured day,
to limp off home to Toyland
where he'll mend, and play, and stay.

Miscast

Oh dear, now I'm a snail.
It always goes like this:
the teacher says, 'Go on, just try'
but things go so amiss.

I really don't like drama,
now I'm longing for the bell.
I always find pretending
drives me back into my shell.

Know your geography

Warm coats aren't needed in Chile,
Greece isn't smeary at all,
Thailand prefers its neck open,
Turkey has no distinct call.

Finland's not fond of the water
To my knowledge Wales doesn't wail.
And which ignoramus said Greenland
is so called because it's gone stale?

Miracle
world

Old friends

On an ordinary jungle day
a funny thing took place,
a meeting of such opposites
in a hollow, hemmed-in space.

In the old trunk of a wrinkled tree
a gorilla of some size
saw a caterpillar on his nose,
when he crossed his eyes.

The gorilla's name was Binbag,
the caterpillar's Bjork,
and with introductions over
they then began to talk

about themselves, and books they'd written
on quiet evenings in,
but sadly never published
as the plots were somewhat thin.

They talked of hopes not happened,
of living different days.
Of, perhaps, exotic travels
to Walton on the Naze.

They talked of swapping places
and wondered if they'd dare.
Bjork got quite excited
at the thought of having fur.

'Then you could crawl in places
that you've never seen before.
And I could yawn and show my teeth
and beat my chest and roar.'

They talked of times that troubled,
of things that sometimes died.
Of often being frightened
and being forced to hide.

They talked of things imagined,
of mornings without hours.
They talked of things miraculous,
the energy of flowers.

And the silence of a sunset,
how dozens come in twelves,
and through speaking to each other
they learned more about themselves.

And what they learned was ancient,
much older than us now –
gorillas, caterpillars
hold the breath of love somehow.

Dual purpose

A larva is a marvel
but take the 'r' away
it then pours from volcanoes
when spelled l-a-v-a

A larva is a wonder
that's been delicately rolled –
a parasol of colours.
A butterfly on hold.

Snow

Things are often described
'as white as' you.
You are very rarely
like something else.
And when you land,
and become spread out,
the streets go dense
with quiet.
It is as if you make us
listen and be glad.

When we roll in you,
scoop you up
and scatter you,
when we mound you
and build in you,
when we lie in you
on our backs
sweeping our arms
leaving the imprint of wings,
you do become something else –

Because we imagine that angels
are shaped rather like us
but taller and glowing,
still with nostrils and ankles,
blowing bugles
and not getting told off,
and, obviously,
with wings.

But what if all along
it turned out
that you are an angel
bringing a message
of stillness
from a vast, pure place.

And when you melt
on pavements
and in fields,
what you are doing
is taking off,
but in stages.

Maybe that is why
your rising
and disappearing
make us so pray to you
from here below
'... Don't go snow,
please don't go...'

Talking to
Mrs Thomas

I'd rather not...

I've got a bad knee
and I may fall over
and make it badder.

If I could sit at the back
and read a book, or draw.
I'd be so quiet
you wouldn't know I was there.
... Well obviously if you looked up I would be
  there,
but if you didn't, look up that is, you wouldn't
  know I was... there.

I'd rather not go into the playground,
  Mrs Thomas.
No, I don't think I'm trying to tell you something
but it looks like rain
and it will be such a bother
for you to send me out there
only to have to bring me back in again.
It hardly seems worth it.
So if I sit over by the radiator
and start drying off now
we'll be ahead of ourselves, won't we?
That would be quite good, wouldn't it?

I'd rather not go into the playground,
  Mrs Thomas.
No, nothing's frightening me much…
… My father said you've got to stand up for
  yourself,
so that's quite good isn't it, Mrs Thomas?

You're going to the staff room to do some
  marking…
… can I come with you, please?

I'd rather not go into the playground,
  Mrs Thomas.
Please don't make me go into the playground,
  Mrs Thomas.

I wonder where...?

Mrs Thomas, there's a question
I would like to ask you.
It's been troubling me lots
… that's a very nice brooch you're wearing…
the question is, where do we go when we die?

I've asked lots of people.
I asked my brother
but he was off out.
My mother didn't know
and my father didn't care.
I asked one of the dinner ladies
but I think the question upset her.
I even asked our dog,
he just wagged his tail
which is one way of looking at it.

Why I'm asking is that my grandmother
died last week and she's gone to Plymouth.
I couldn't go because it was too far
but everyone said it was a very nice service.
It was where she wanted to go
because that's where she came from.

Mrs Thomas, what do you think?
Where do we end up?
… Where we've always wanted to go…
… Not Plymouth… Somewhere bigger…

I wonder where that is then?

Class project

Mrs Thomas said we had to write
about a thunderstorm... so here goes...

bang rattling... loud and frightening
not much warning... clouds fighting
drinks spilt... *torrential rain*
everything soaked... especially the sofa
God playing the drums... neighbours
  complained
music much too loud... room booming
I didn't like it... so hid in the shed
police came... names taken
parents were away... they would never have
  allowed it
when will this storm end? ... been going on
  for days
social worker's been; ... she went to Florida
  once
huge thunderstorms there... but they stop
  after a while

'Mrs Thomas, here's my project. You know
you said to write about a thunderstorm, well
I have. It happened in our house when my older
brother had a party.'

The Adventures of Just A Mo the Eskimo and Mrs Just A Mo

Episode 1: An incredible journey

Just A Mo the Eskimo
swam all the way to Norway,
which turned out such a nuisance
as he should have gone to Torbay
to an Eskimo convention
to hear speeches about fish,
but he ended up in fjords
going 'splash' and 'splosh' and 'splish'.

When he got back home again
there was Mrs Just A Mo
who hadn't had his postcard
so how was she to know
that her husband went the wrong way
as he didn't make that clear.
When she asked, 'How was the visit?'
He said, 'Fine, but lots of reindeer.'

This puzzled Mrs Just A Mo,
she imagined that Torbay
had palm trees, beaches, volley ball,
and sun day after day
with deckchairs, rock and candyfloss,
and perhaps a promenade.
She never thought in Torbay that
it rained, and rained quite hard.

She said to her beloved
as they drew hearts in the ice
'The constant rain, dear, over there
could not have been that nice.'
'Oh, not that bad,' said Just A Mo,
'but when the reindeer snorts
the thought occurred to me, maybe
that reindeer's out of sorts.'

'Snorting rain!' said Mrs Mo,
'that's not the place for me!'
They said no more about it
and had frozen chips for tea.

Episode 2: Small miracles

Just A Mo has got a job
on premises quite near,
although it's only seasonal,
a good end to the year.

It's a post with Father Christmas
in a warehouse made of lights
it's a worthwhile occupation
but it does mean working nights.

It's not the main headquarters,
that one's miles away
where someone makes decisions
about profits, plans and pay.

But Just A Mo ignores all this –
from his bench at The North Pole
he sends out shimmering presents
which he's wrapped up with his soul.

He works alongside leprechauns,
pixies, sprites and hobs
and though the work is temporary,
for now, they've all got jobs

Then Christmas Eve when work is done,
with tinsel packed away,
whilst in the sky above them
their employer's loaded sleigh

heads off to distant cities,
some tropically warm,
Just A Mo invites friends home
through the freezing storm

where Mrs Just A Mo has cooked
a special, Yuletide dish
complete with frosted trimmings,
a massive Christmas fish.

Though each one there has been laid off,
on finishing their feast,
they hold a midnight service
and sing carols to the East.

Episode 3: A good idea at the time

Just A Mo's been reading
magazines about
DIY improvements
which teach him how to grout
bathroom, shower and kitchen.
But Just A Mo was keen
on building something that
a polar bear has never seen.

He posted off his order
and several days went by
then a parachute descended
from a cold, clear sky.
Attached to it a huge flat-pack,
an oblong mystery.
What Just A Mo had purchased
was a grand conservatory.

Now Mrs Just A Mo was unaware
of this great scheme,
her cosy igloo was to her
a snug and sheltered dream.
The loo was white and sparkling
whilst the ig was full of grace.
(I should explain that ig's
a wintry word for 'open space'.)

She heard the dreadful clanging
shattering the quiet.
My goodness! she thought, dashing out,
I hope that's not a riot.
Our world is one of silence.
Our doors do not need locks.
Our loudest sound
is the heartbeat of the Arctic fox.

And there she found her Just A Mo
in a dreadful mess,
overwhelmed by everything
and bleating in distress.
Nothing fitted anywhere,
not bracket, glass or screw.
The more he banged and hammered,
the more the problem grew.

'Oh, Mrs Just A Mo', he cried,
'my heart is now so grey.
This was your birthday present
where you could sit and play.
And with your brand new telescope
study when the sky
is ready to tell both of us –
"today's the day you fly".'

'Oh, my poor darling Just A Mo
this really was so kind
but what I say in times like these
is 'whoops' and 'never mind'.
It's good you didn't build it,
it would have been too tall.
The sun through glass to igloo
would have melted the back wall.'

'Oh, lumme', mumbled Just A Mo,
'I'm really duff at this.
I'll go and do some dusting,
but at that I'm hit and miss.'
So then they both went back indoors
and all once more was hush.
And tea was ice-cream sandwiches
and strawberry-flavoured slush.

Episode 4: Worship

It's the lilac sky of morning
in which Just A Mo believes

And from dazzling spreads of starlight
Just A Mo receives
an evening confirmation
that all his world feels right

Made clearer, cleaner, constant
by the blizzards of the night

The Final Episode:
Just A Mo's love song
to Mrs Just A Mo

You are the hush
the heart and the heat
in all this territory

You are my fortune
my treasure and peace
you are my jubilee

A trio of limericks

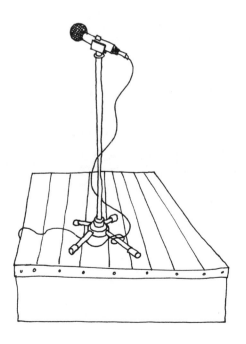

A limerick

There was a hip rapper called 'Bass'
who was crucial, and happenin', and ace
he wore baggy and 'bad'
but his pad was quite trad
with a bedspread of Nottingham lace.

Another limerick

This spaceman got terribly fraught
and blamed it on how he was taught
cash for his crashed rocket
came out of his pocket
now his bank balance shows astro-nought.

Another other limerick

A nondescript squirrel called Wayne
has this vast, mathematical brain
every acorn that's been
he has counted, and seen,
something oak trees can never explain.